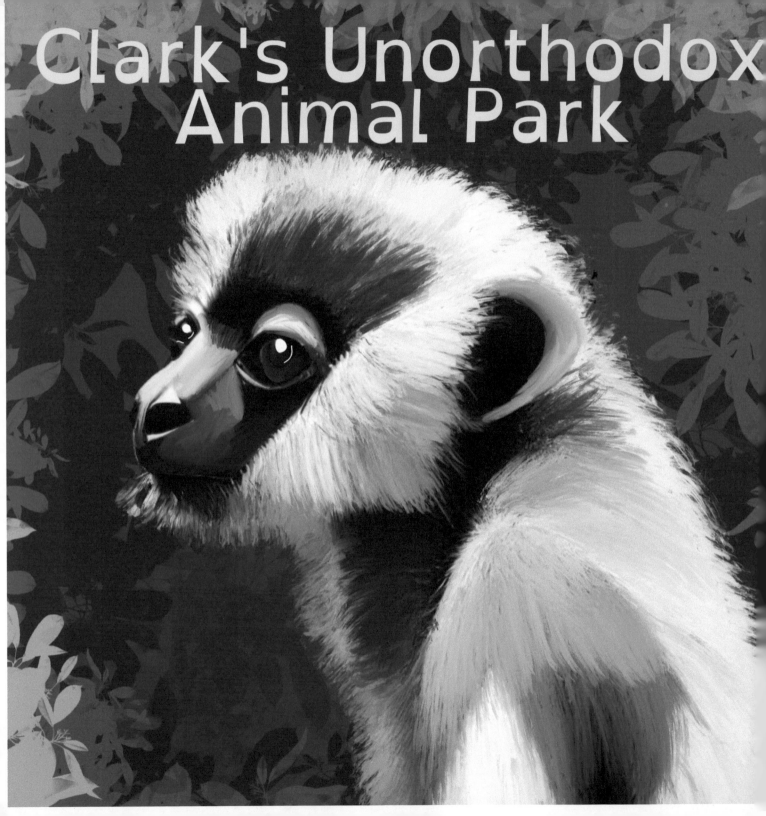

Clark's Unorthodox
Animal Park

Clark's Unorthodox Animal Park

For my brother Blake, who has loved animals far more than people all his life, and helped me discover some new ones for this story. For my sister, Jordan, who is still upset Blake took her place as the "animal kid" in the family, and knows far more animal facts than I. For my brother Clark, who cannot read.

A special thank you to Kobe, my anonymous aunt, Deeda, Rhi & Jess, Lil R and Mama S. Also, thank you to my parents, Dan and Karina, for encouraging me to follow my passions wherever they take me.

This font was chose for kids like Jordan and Blake, as it is made to help those with dyslexia read. I hope this helps children struggling with dyslexia enjoy reading, and this story, a little more than they would have without it.

Now let's see what Clark has to teach us today...

Blake and Terry the Toad.

There was a lover of animals, his name was Blake. He loved all animal types, make no mistake.

Blake had a sister, Jordan, who loved animals, too! They studied all species, some old and some new.

Jordan with a snake!

Unlike other kids,
after school they
would not play.
They would look for
animals, and watch
them all day!

Their dogs, Toopy and Butch!

A brown spider from
Grandma Wendy's basement!

Their classmates
would see arachnids
and run,
but they thought
seeing spiders spin
webs was so fun!

The Big Book of Bogus Beasts

A book full of imaginary (but awesome) animals!

One day their parent's told them of a place where odd animals roamed, where peculiar was embraced.

They packed up their bags, and hopped in the car. It was a really long day, they drove very far!

Hittin' the road!

Soon they arrived, right after dark! There it was, Clark's Unorthodox Animal Park! Clark also loves animals and keeping them safe.

The park entrance!

Hey look! It's Clark!

That is why he created this place! What animals lived here, Blake did not know. Jordan couldn't wait for her knowledge to grow!

Albatross (al·buh·traas): 21/22 species are approaching extinction.

Inside they met an Albatross, a very cool bird. It had the largest wingspan they had ever heard!

Binturong was next, a name few people know. They smell like popcorn and put on quite a show!

The binturong (bin·tr·ong) is a vulnerable species.

What's Kopi Luwak (kow·pee loo·wuk)? It's coffee from poo! Civets eat the coffee beans, then people drink them, too!

Civet (si·vuht): Some species are vulnerable and endangered.

The dhole (dowl) is an endangered species.

Dholes are quite cute, and can jump 7 feet in the air! There are not many left in the wild, so Clark brought some there.

Echidnas (uh·kid·na·s) are critically endangered.

They saw Echnidnas next, mammals with no teeth! Jordan met a cute one and named him Keith.

F is for Fennec Fox, a large-eared mammal. They live in the desert, just like a camel!

The Fennec (feh·nuhk) Fox lives in burrows with up to 12 other!

Gharials love to blow bubbles through their snout. They are nocturnal- at night they roam about!

Gharials (geh·ree·uhl·s) are critically endangered.

The Hoatzin (howt·zin) will mate for life and raise 2-5 chicks!

A Hoatzin, what's that? It's a bird that is smelly. They digest food uniquely and have more than one belly!

The Indri (in-dree) is critically endangered.

An Indri, you say? Look at it's fur! "They are cute" Jordan says, "like a big lemur!".

Next, they saw a Jerboa, with long legs and big ears. Clark told them they must protect this species, before it dissappears!

The Long-eared Jerboa (jer·bow·uh) is an endangered species.

A Kinkajou spreads pollen from flower to flower! They steal honey from bees, and find fruit to devour.

The Kinkajou (kink·uh·joo) is also known as a "Honey Bear"!

All species of the Slow Loris (law·ris) are vulnerable or endangered.

This is the Loris, they have huge eyes to see in the night! They lick their elbow glands to make venom, and deliver a deadly bite!

The mandrill (man·druhl) is a vulnerable species.

A Mandrill is a massive monkey with a bright coloured nose. This quadruped uses four limbs, wherever it goes!

Numbats (nuhm·baat·s) are an endangered species.

Next, Blake spotted a Numbat, with a long sticky tongue. They use it to eat termites, and have a pouch for their young!

The Okapis were cool, with their zebra-like rears. They have long tongues to clean both their eyes and ears.

Okapis (oh·kaa·pee) are endangered.

One quarter (1/4) of Pangolin (pang·guh·luhn) species are critically endangered.

Jordan loved the Pangolins, with their interesting tails! These pinecone-like creatures have keratin scales.

The quetzal's (kuht·saal) population is decreasing.

The Quetzal was next, a colourful bird! They nest in rotten trees, isn't that absurd?

A Red Tegu is a big ol' lizard, who loves to go for swims. Some tegus can walk using just their back limbs!

Red Tegus (teh·goo·s) can grow 3-5 feet in length!

A Saiga is an antelope with an incredible nose. It filters out dust, wherever it goes.

Saigas (sai·guh·s) are critically endangered.

Tapirs (tay·per·s) are a vulnerable species.

Tapirs are cool and can eat a lot in one day! They camouflage their young so they don't become prey.

The Long-wattled Umbrellabird is vulnerable.

Look at it's hat! Well that's absurd. There are actually three species of Umbrellabird.

Verreaux's Sifaka, a relative of the lemur, can jump 30 feet. This lets them find leaves, fruits and nuts up high to eat.

The Verreaux's (ver·oh·s) Sifaka (suh·faa·kuh) is endangered.

A Wolffish was spotted while swimming past. This 5 foot long fish can crunch critters fast.

The Wolffish (wulf·fish) is at risk of becoming extinct.

The Xerus (zur·uhs) is 4 species of African Ground Squirrel.

A Xerus from Africa... what did that say? It's big fluffy tail shades it from the sun all day.

The Yabby (ya·bee) is a vulnerable species.

A Yabby is a freshwater crustacean. They are from Australia and have a decreasing population.

The last that they saw, was a little group of Zokors, similar to moles. They have sensitive eyes, and sharp claws for digging holes.

The Chinese Zokor (Zo·ker) is a threatened species.

The park was magnificent, quite a sight to see! But why are they endangered? Can we help? You and Me?

Fires and deforestation can ruin natural habitats!

Thankfully 100+ countries aim to end deforestation by 2030!

This park is a start, a place for them to roam. Humans destroy many habitats, and they lose their homes.

Ask your parents to help learn about animal conservation in your area!

Do not fret, for there is lots we can do! Support animal conservation, and share their story too!

The animals need help, but we can save them all. It doesn't matter your age, how big or how small.

Some kids cleaning up their local park!

When they went home they remembered to recycle, to never leave trash on the ground. They made many posters, to spread the word around!

If you see this symbol on something don't throw it out! It can be used to make new things!

Look how beautiful! Have you seen a clean beach before?

They cared for the planet, the birds and the bees.
They wanted to save the forests, and clean the seas.

Soon, more children joined and helped spread the word. Then something amazing occurred! The species at risk were running free! Safe from unnatural threats, thanks to you and me.

When we work together, we can cause a spark! The animals were saved thanks to you, me, and Clark's Unorthodox Animal Park!

CPSIA information can be obtained
at www.ICGtesting.com
Printed in the USA
LVHW071255021222
734355LV00002B/19